Mr Bill
and the
Runaway Sausag

MR BILL AND THE RUNAWAY SAUSAGES
A PICTURE CORGI 0 552 52310 0

PRINTING HISTORY
First published by Blackie and Son Ltd. 1983
Picture Corgi edition published 1986
Reprinted 1987, 1988, 1989.

Picture Corgi Books are published by
Transworld Publishers Ltd., 61-63 Uxbridge Road,
Ealing, London W5 5SA.

Printed and bound in Portugal by Printer Portuguesa.

Mr. Bill and the Runaway Sausages

Georgie Adams

Pictures by Margaret Chamberlain

PICTURE CORGI

This is a story about Mr Bill, who lives with his wife Mrs Bill and their young son Ben. They have a black cat called Kitty Mitty and a shaggy mongrel called Micky Mutton. Mr Bill, Mrs Bill, Ben, Kitty Mitty and Micky Mutton all live together in a round pink house called Pork Pie Cottage.

Every day Mr Bill gets up early. Mrs Bill gets up early too.
She cooks him a delicious breakfast of
sausages,
sausages,
and sausages.
They are particularly tasty sausages
because Mrs Bill makes them herself.

And every day Mr Bill sells
pounds
and pounds
and pounds
of Mrs Bill's sausages in his grocer's shop.

People come from miles around to buy them.
Mr Bill is quite famous for them.

At nine o'clock every morning Mr Bill opens his shop
and
tramp, tramp
chatter, chatter,
push, push,
Mr Bill's customers come bustling in.

What a noise!
All those people talking at once.
What a squeeze!
Mr Bill's shop is rather small and some of
his customers are rather . . . large.

Then one Saturday morning something really awful happened.
Mrs Bill caught a cold.
Sneeze, sneeze,
cough, cough,
snuffle, snuffle.

She couldn't get out of bed.
She couldn't make any sausages!
"Never mind," said Mr Bill and he went
downstairs to make Mrs Bill a nice cup of tea.

When Mr Bill opened his shop that morning
he hung a notice on the door.
It said: SORRY. NO SAUSAGES TODAY.
Goodness, his customers were cross.
Puff, puff,
Tut, tut,
Dear, dear!
"What, no sausages?" they cried.
"How inconvenient," said one.
"It's an outrage!" said another.
What a greedy, ungrateful lot they were.
No one seemed to care about poor Mrs Bill
in bed with a cold.
And they went away.

"Oh dear," sighed Mr Bill. "I have lost all my customers."
Just then a travelling salesman came into the shop.
"Good morning, good morning, good morning!" said the salesman.
"Would you like to buy a television set?"
"No thank you," said Mr Bill.
"How about a vacuum cleaner?"
"Not today," said Mr Bill.

"Well then," said the salesman, "how about a packet of Instant Super Sausage Mix? It's on special offer this week."
"INSTANT SUPER SAUSAGE MIX!" cried Mr Bill.
"New and improved," smiled the salesman. "Just add water," he said, tapping the side of the packet with his finger.
"I'll take the lot!" said Mr Bill.

"Quick, Ben!" cried Mr Bill as he ran next door to the cottage. "Come and help!"
Ben ran into the kitchen and found his mother's largest mixing bowl.
Mr Bill filled a bucket with water.
Kitty Mitty and Micky Mutton looked on with interest.
Ben poured packets and packets of Instant Super Sausage Mix into the mixing bowl, while Mr Bill mixed in the water with a large wooden spoon.
Stir, stir,
Slup, slup,
Splosh, splosh.

before Mrs Bill could stick her foot out to stop them
they were out through the door, into the passage and
out of an open window.
"Oh no!" wailed Mr Bill. "We'll never catch them now.
They'll be all over the town in no time."
Which was true.

Strings
and strings
and strings
of Instant Super Sausages bounded
out onto the pavement and tumbled
down the street.

They got under people's feet,
wound themselves round lamp posts,
got inside letter-boxes,
climbed trees.

"What now?" said Ben, peering at the sticky mixture.
Mr Bill looked at the instructions.
"It says wait five seconds for the mixture to work," said Mr Bill.
Ben counted slowly on his fingers,
"One – two – three – four – five . . ."
The mixing bowl began to tremble.
Then it began to shake.

And before Ben or Mr Bill could say another word,
hundreds and hundreds of Instant Super Sausages
began tumbling out of the mixing bowl
onto the table and across the floor.

"Do something, Dad!" cried Ben, who was now
up to his knees in sausages.
Just then Mrs Bill came downstairs in her
dressing-gown to see what all the fuss was about.
"Whatever is going on?" she said as she opened the door.
Well, those sausages saw their chance to escape and

Slid down
drainpipes,
hopped on buses
and swung on telephone
wires.
And lots of other things besides, which made
the townsfolk very cross indeed.

It hadn't taken Micky Mutton long to discover
that he wasn't dreaming.
He had rushed out of the house, his nose tingling
with excitement.
Very soon he met some friends;
big dogs,
small dogs,
stuffy dogs
and scruffy dogs.

Round and round the town they ran.
All afternoon.
Dogs chasing sausages,
sausages chasing people,
people chasing sausages,
sausages chasing dogs!

By Saturday tea-time everyone was exhausted.
Even the sausages were beginning to look a
little
worse for wear.

Then one string of sausages discovered
the Railway Station. There was a
goods train standing
at the platform with
trucks
and trucks
and trucks
waiting to be loaded. Quite empty.

The first string of sausages hopped aboard. So did another and another until the trucks were full of fat little sausages all eager for a ride.
The guard waved his flag.
The station master blew his whistle and the train puffed out of sight.

And that is the end of the story except to say that Mr Bill doesn't have a grocer's shop any more.
He's opened a flower shop instead!
And Mrs Bill doesn't make sausages any more.
She grows chrysanthemums instead.

Mr Bill sells
bunches
and bunches
of Mrs Bill's chrysanthemums in his shop.
He is quite famous for them.